107¾
Elephant Jokes

107¾ Elephant Jokes

written and illustrated by

Jack Stokes

Doubleday & Company, Inc., Garden City, New York

ISBN 0-385-14101-7 Trade
       0-385-14102-5 Prebound
Library of Congress Catalog Card Number 78–1223
Copyright © 1979 by Jack Stokes
All Rights Reserved
Printed in the United States of America
9 8 7 6 5 4 3 2

Dedicated to John H. Felber

*Without his help, going insane
would be much more difficult.*

What do you call five hundred elephants at a concert?

The audience.

What do you get if you cross an elephant with a mouse?

Very large holes in your baseboard.

Why don't elephants wear shoes?

They can't tie the laces on their back feet when they have shoes on their front feet.

Why don't elephants like turnips?

For the same reasons that no one likes turnips.

Why don't elephants fly?

Airline tickets are too expensive.

Why don't elephants cross their eyes?

Because i's are dotted; t's are crossed.

When does an elephant charge?

When he doesn't have cash.

Can elephants see at night?

Not with their eyes shut.

Why can't elephants sing?

*Maybe they can but they don't want to be
    mistaken for birds.*

*What do you have when you cross an elephant
    with a skunk?*

Very few friends.

*What do you do when an elephant has hay
    fever?*

Keep about a mile away.

*How do you keep an elephant from getting
    angry?*

You better find out.

Why do so many elephants live in zoos?

It's cheaper than apartment houses.

Why don't elephants close the refrigerator door?

They are afraid with the light out.

What happened when the elephant took a bus?

He got arrested and they made him return it.

How can you tell an elephant from a bowl of potato salad?

If you can't do that, don't come to my picnic.

What does an elephant do for a cold?

He probably doesn't want one, so don't offer.

Why don't elephants play basketball?

You can't find five elephants who are willing to have purple trunks.

Why don't elephants like grass houses?

The beams are hard to chew.

Why aren't elephants square?

Some of the old fuddy-duddies are.

Why don't elephants lay eggs?

They can't get into birdhouses.

Why don't elephants have feathers?

It would confuse duck hunters.

What would happen if elephants had feathers?

At molting season you'd have feathers up to your armpits.

What else would happen if elephants had feathers?

Pillows would be a lot cheaper.

What do you get if you cross an elephant with a rabbit?

*Whatever it is, you are going to have a couple
of hundred more in a few months!*

Why do elephants wear ice skates?

Because they can't play hockey very well on skis.

Where are elephants found?

Where they were lost, usually.

How do you fill an elephant's tooth?

Very quickly.

How can you tell if there's an elephant in the back seat of your car?

If the front wheels don't touch the road and someone keeps stealing your peanuts, it's probably an elephant.

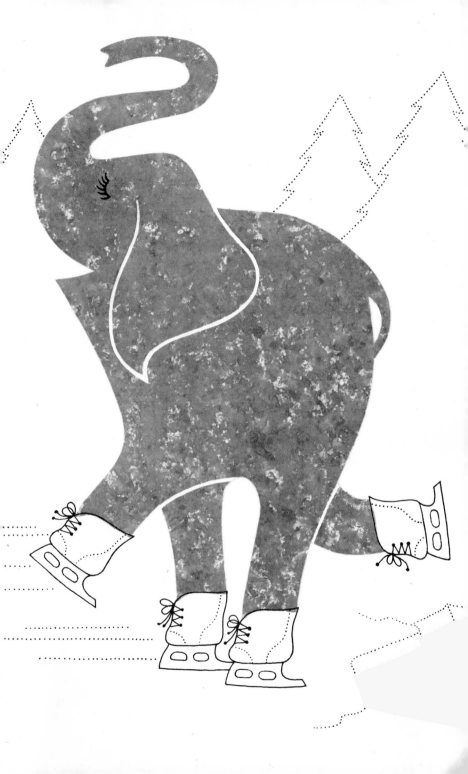

Why are elephants vegetarians?

Who can afford 125 pounds of hamburger every day?

What do you get if you cross an elephant with an alligator?

A stylish but very expensive trunk.

Why did the elephant buy a blond wig?

She was tired of her red wig.

Why don't elephants go to costume parties?

They're not usually asked.

Why don't drunks see blue elephants?

Blue elephants aren't allowed in bars.

Why did the elephant take geometry?

Because the algebra class was full.

Where does a ten-ton elephant sleep?

Anywhere he wants.

What do you get when you cross an elephant with a kangaroo?

Big dents in the ground.

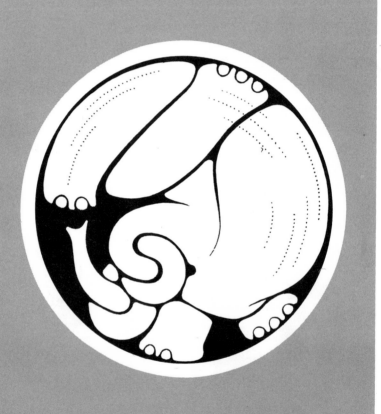

Why don't elephants buy ten-speed bikes?

They can't use hand brakes.

Why don't elephants use automatic clothes dryers?

Their trunks get all tangled up.

Why don't elephants have long toenails?

Because they are cheap-looking.

Why don't elephants wear purple coats?

They don't want to be mistaken for grapes.

What do you get if you cross an elephant with an ant?

Whatever you call it—it only takes one to ruin a picnic.

Do you think an elephant looks silly wearing pearls?

Not if she's wearing a black dress.

What do you get if you cross an elephant with a beaver?

Hoover Dam.

Why don't elephants use typewriters competently?

Some can, but most of them don't like to capitalize on it.

Why don't elephants wear high heels?

They think they already have pretty ankles.

Why do elephants need trunks?

*Because most beaches won't let them in
    without them.*

Why don't elephants wear bikinis?

Because they already have trunks.

Why don't elephants smoke?

They do if they're lit.

Why do elephants have good memories?

I forget. I'm not an elephant.

Why did the elephant wear silver earrings?

Because gold was too expensive.

Why do elephants paint their toenails red?

To hide in cherry trees.

*Why haven't you ever seen an elephant
    in a cherry tree?*

Because it works!

Why don't elephants eat fruit cocktail?

They think the cherries are toenails.

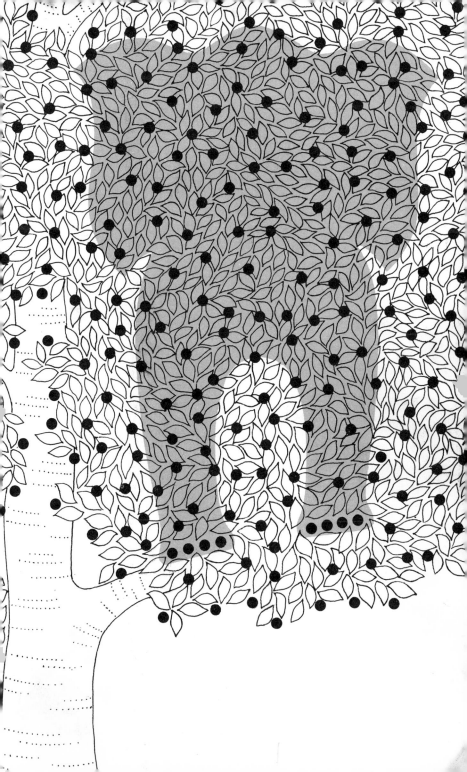

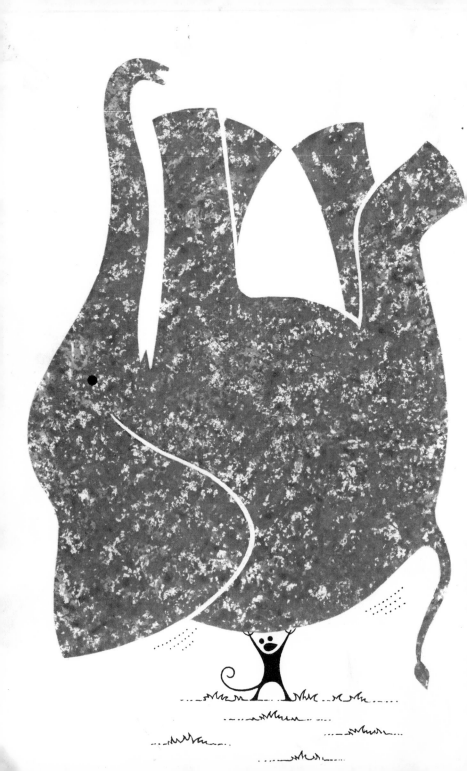

Why did the elephant go charging through the airport?

They got his trunk on the wrong flight.

Why don't elephants wear knickers?

No one wears knickers anymore.

Why did the elephant learn to play the saxophone?

He was tired of trumpeting.

What do you call a mouse that can pick up an elephant?

Sir.

Why don't elephants water-ski?

Very few own boats.

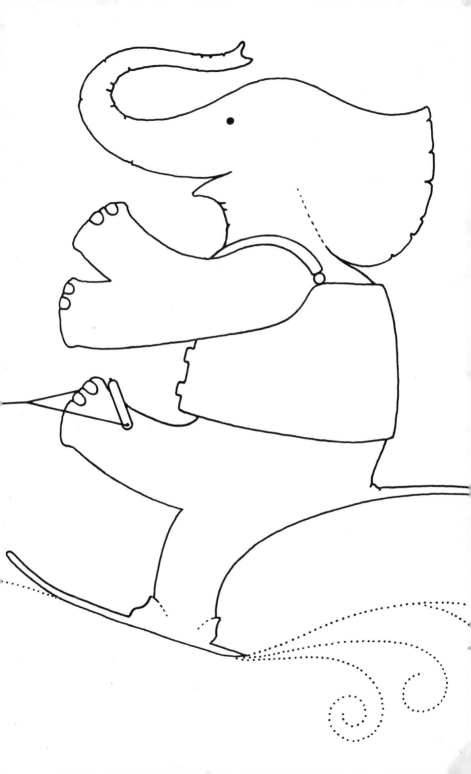

What do you get when you cross an elephant with a Frisbee?

A hernia.

Why do elephants wear red earmuffs?

Because white gets dirty too quickly.

How can you tell if an elephant has slept in your bed?

Look for peanut shells under the pillow.

Why do elephants spray water on themselves?

They can't get into stall showers.

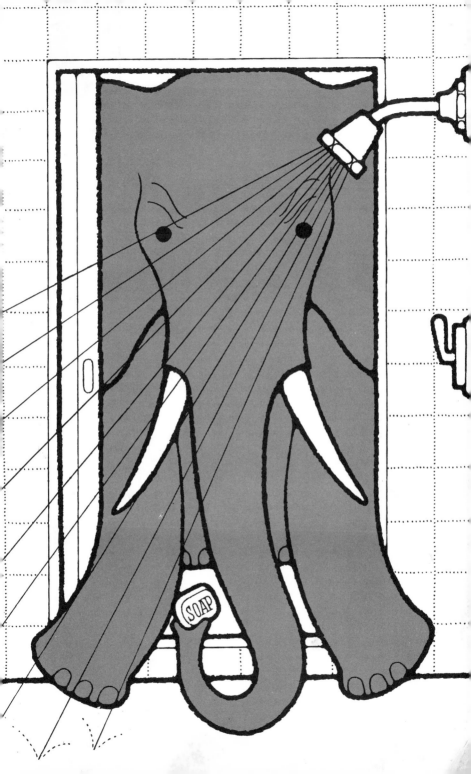

Why don't elephants like beer?

Who said they don't?

Why did the elephant drive to New York?

Because they wouldn't take a trunk on the plane.

Why don't you see elephants in elevators?

Because they hide in the back corner.

How can you tell an elephant from a giraffe?

Say, "Hi, giraffe," and if he doesn't look up, he's probably an elephant.

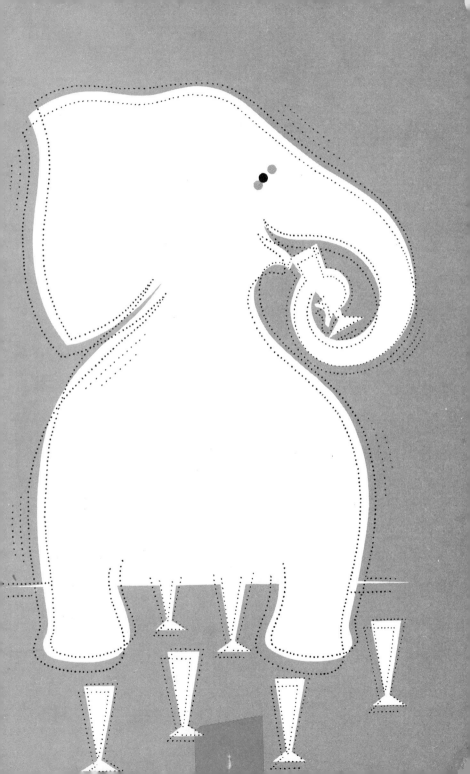

How do you know when there are alligators around?

The elephants have very short trunks.

What do you get if you cross an elephant with a dairy cow?

How do you think they make peanut butter?

Why don't elephants do the minuet?

Orchestras don't play minuets anymore.

Why did the elephant wear horn-rimmed glasses?

Because he didn't like contact lenses.

Why don't elephants take subway trains?

They are too hard to carry up the stairs.

*What do you get if you cross an elephant
      with a light bulb?*

A huge electric bill.

What's a good elephant's name?

Henry.

Why?

Ask Henry. He's a good elephant.

What do you get if you cross an elephant with a pumpkin?

A huge jack-o'-lantern with a fire extinguisher.

Why don't elephants like mice?

They don't want people to think they're cats.

Why don't elephants wear stockings?

Because panty hose are more comfortable.

Why do elephants live in jungles?

They are too big to live in igloos.

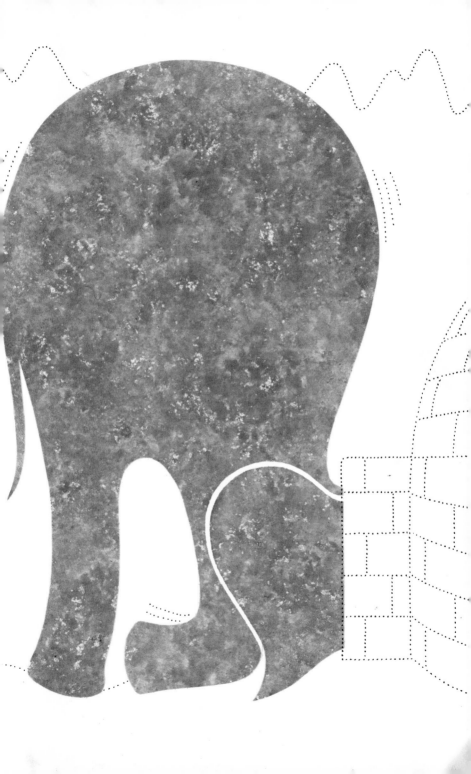

Should you laugh when an elephant tells a
joke?

Unless you enjoy being thrown fifty feet in the
air, you should.

What do you get if you cross an elephant with a
peach?

A three-ton ball of fuzz charging at you.

Why do elephants make good switchboard
operators?

They are great on trunk calls.

Why do elephants wear sneakers?

Coaches won't let them on the gym floor
without them.

8.588

Why don't you ever see an elephant in a gold lamé dress?

Most of them have better taste.

What do you get when you cross an elephant with a parrot?

I'm not sure, but give it a cracker when it wants one!

How can you tell if an elephant took your bicycle?

There are ruts three feet deep in your yard.

How can you tell if an elephant used your toothbrush?

It smells of peanuts.

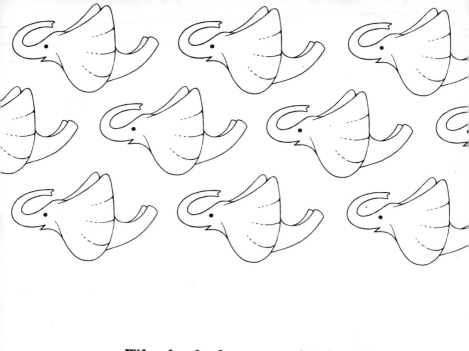

Why do elephants travel in herds?

If they traveled in flocks, they might be mistaken for birds or sheep.

What do you get if you cross an elephant with a Volkswagen?

A car that gets thirty-five miles per bale and washes itself.

What did Jane say when she saw the elephant wearing formal attire?

"It must be after six."

What did Tarzan say?

"Maybe he's our waiter."

What did the elephant say?

"I hope they don't think I'm a penguin."

Why did the elephant call in sick?

No one ever calls in well.

What do you get if you cross an elephant with a sheep?

Enough wool to knit a skyscraper.

Why did the elephant wear green eye shadow?

To go with her green dress.

How can you tell if there's an elephant under your bed?

If you need a ladder to get down and it's not a bunk bed, there may be an elephant under there somewhere.

Where do blue elephants come from?

Unhappy families.

Where do white elephants come from?

Church bazaars.

Where do yellow elephants come from?

Chickens.

How do you kill a yellow elephant?

Say, "Boo!" He'll die of fright.

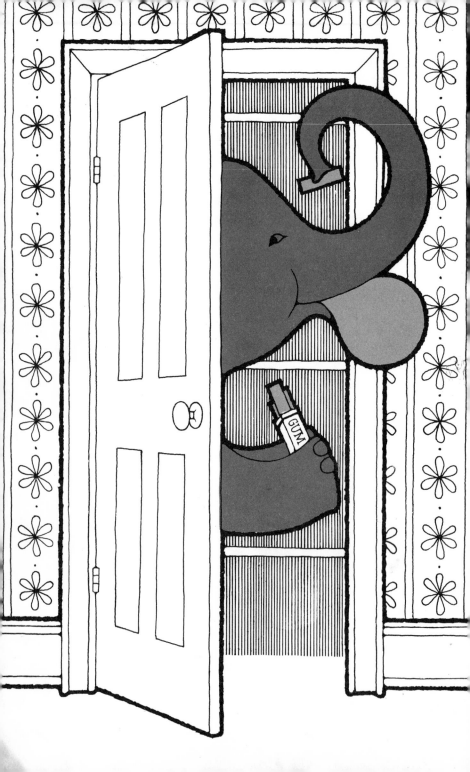

Why do elephants stay home on three-day weekends?

They feel silly going anywhere with a trunk for three days.

What do you get if you cross an elephant with a cat?

Something that purrs as it squashes you.

Why don't elephants chew gum?

Maybe they do, but not in public.

Why don't elephants make good bartenders?

A lot of people stop drinking when they see them.

Why do elephants give themselves showers?

Who else is going to?

What do you get if you cross an elephant with a chicken?

The biggest gray egg you've ever seen.

Why don't a lot of elephants have master's degrees?

There aren't a lot of elephants anymore.

How do you make a birthday cake for an elephant?

First, find a cement mixer . . .

(I promised you ¾ of a joke, didn't I?)

Jack Stokes thinks that a good laugh will keep the rest of your life in better perspective. He was born and raised in Ohio and now lives with his wife and three children in Old Lyme, Connecticut. A free-lance designer and illustrator since 1966, he has done illustrations for advertising as well as for adult and children's publications. He is the author and illustrator of Mind Your A's and Q's, Loony Limericks, Let's Catch a Fish, Let's Make a Kite, Let's Be Nature's Friend, Let's Make Stilts, Let's Make a Toy Sailboat *and has several other books in varying stages of progress. When not writing or illustrating books, Mr. Stokes keeps busy preserving old architecture, puttering at landscaping the yard, and just lying on the beach, where he claims he is thinking up more jokes.*

DATE DUE			
MAR 30			
APR 20			
MAY 11			
DEC 21			
JAN 4			
FEB 1			
MAY 10			

GAYLORD 234

PRINTED IN U. S. A.